BLAZERS

CRIME SOLVERS

BLOOD EVIDENCE

by Amy Kortuem

CAPSTONE PRESS
a capstone imprint

Blazers Books are published by Capstone Press,
1710 Roe Crest Drive, North Mankato, Minnesota 56003
www.mycapstone.com

Library of Congress Cataloging-in-Publication Data
Names: Kortuem, Amy, author.
Title: Blood evidence / by Amy Kortuem.
Description: North Mankato, Minnesota : Capstone Press, [2019] | Series:
   Blazers. Crime solvers | Includes index.
Identifiers: LCCN 2018001962 (print) | LCCN 2018008184 (ebook) | ISBN
   9781543529951 (eBook PDF) | ISBN 9781543529876 (hardcover) | ISBN
   9781543529913 (pbk.)
Subjects: LCSH: Forensic biology—Juvenile literature. |
   Blood—Analysis—Juvenile literature. | Evidence, Criminal—Juvenile
   literature. | Criminal investigation—Juvenile literature.
Classification: LCC QH313.5.F67 (ebook) | LCC QH313.5.F67 K67 2019 (print) |
   DDC 363.25/62—dc23
LC record available at https://lccn.loc.gov/2018001962

Editorial Credits
Carrie Braulick Sheely, editor; Kayla Rossow, designer;
Svetlana Zhurkin, media researcher; Kris Wilfahrt, production specialist

Photo Credits
Alamy: Mikael Karlsson, 13; Getty Images: PNC, 29; iStockphoto: D-Keine, 23,
Yuri_Arcurs, 6; Shutterstock: adriaticfoto, 25, akepong srichaichana, 21, Andrew
Trooman, 18, Chaikom, 16, Corepics VOF, 15 (top), 20, Couperfield, cover, 10, 14,
15 (bottom), Daria Serdtseva, 26, Himchenko.E, 12, irin-k, 22, Olga Nikonova, 17,
Syda Productions, 5, Zoka74, 9

Design Elements by Shutterstock

Printed in the United States.
PA017

TABLE OF CONTENTS

Chapter 1
At the Crime Scene **4**

Chapter 2
Finding and Collecting Blood **8**

Chapter 3
Bloodstain Patterns **16**

Chapter 4
Using Blood Evidence **24**

Glossary 30

Read More 31

Internet Sites... 31

Critical Thinking Questions 32

Index 32

AT THE CRIME SCENE

People living in an apartment call the police. They have found their neighbor dead. Crime **scene** investigators (CSIs) arrive quickly. They look for clues.

scene—the place of an event or action

CSIs may take pictures to record the clues they find.

FACT

Your body contains about
1.5 gallons (5.7 liters) of blood.

The CSIs find blood. They use cotton swabs to collect it. Tests show most of the blood is from the **victim**. But a small amount is from a known **criminal**. Blood **evidence** helps solve another crime.

victim—a person who is hurt, killed, or made to suffer because of a disaster, accident, or crime

criminal—someone who commits a crime

evidence—information, items, and facts that help prove something is true or false

CHAPTER 2

FINDING AND COLLECTING BLOOD

CSIs can see some blood easily. They use **chemicals** and tools to find blood they can't see. CSIs can make blood show up that is many years old.

chemical—a substance used in or produced by chemistry

CSIs may find transfer bloodstains. This happens when blood moves onto another object. Bloody shoe prints are transfer bloodstains.

A CSI uses an ultraviolet (UV) light to search for bloodstains.

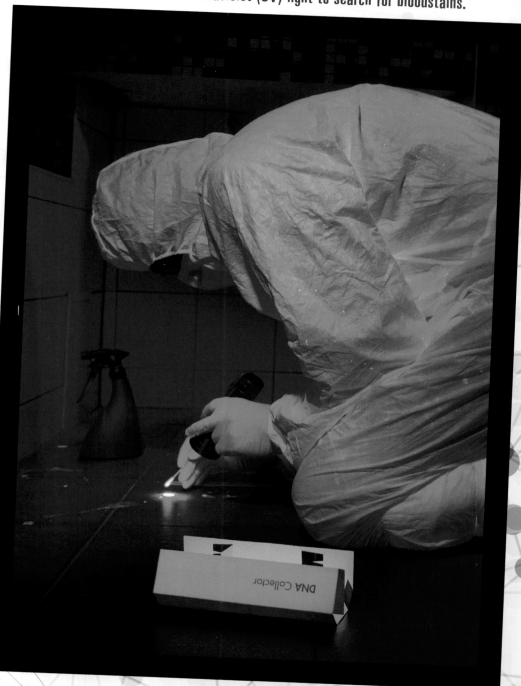

DNA Collector

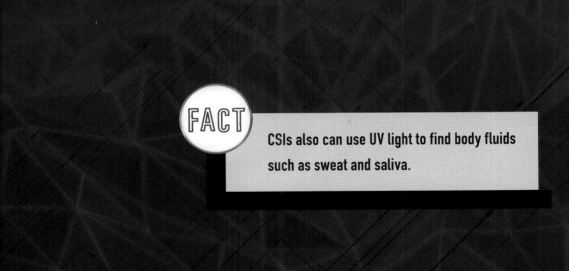

FACT

CSIs also can use UV light to find body fluids such as sweat and saliva.

CSIs can use special lights to find bloodstains. If a stain shows up, they take a blood sample with a cotton swab. They spray the swab with a chemical. The swab turns pink if there is blood.

CSIs sometimes spray chemicals on large areas to find blood. Luminol makes bloodstains glow blue. Other chemicals turn bloodstains yellow-green or purple.

FACT

Sometimes blood looks blue when light shines on our skin and veins. But it is always red.

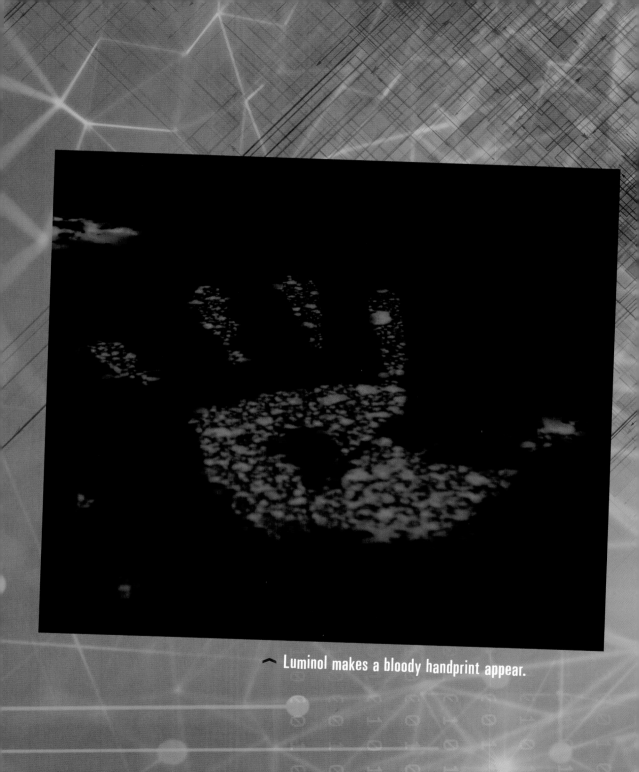

Luminol makes a bloody handprint appear.

CSIs must **record** what they find at crime scenes. They take pictures of bloodstains. They use cotton swabs to collect wet blood. They scrape dried blood into paper containers. They may take bloody objects to the crime lab.

record—to show evidence of something

Photos can show where evidence was located at the scene.

CSIs collect wet blood with cotton swabs. They allow it to dry before taking it to the lab.

CHAPTER 3

BLOODSTAIN PATTERNS

CSIs also study bloodstain patterns. When a blood drop falls, it forms a shape. A drop falling a short way leaves a thick, round stain. It will have a smooth edge. A drop that falls farther will have a **crown**.

❮ blood drops without crowns

crown—a jagged edge on a blood drop

blood drops with crowns

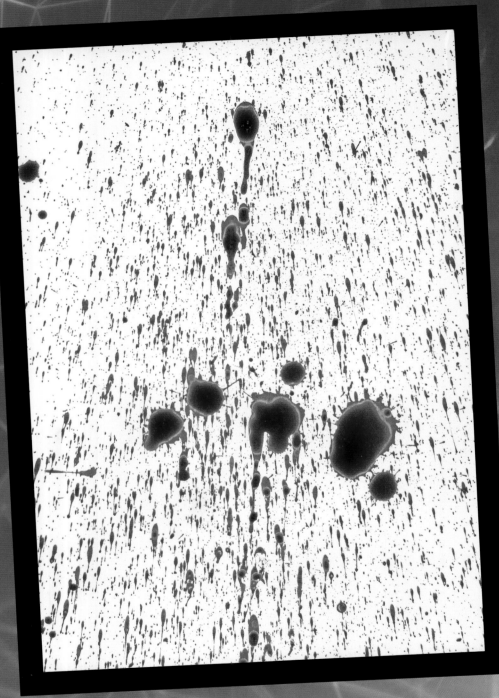

^ blood drops with tails

Blood falls at an angle from a moving person who is bleeding. A "tail" forms at one end. The tail points away from the direction of travel. These drops help CSIs know where the person went.

Cuts, **bullet** wounds, and physical attacks can cause **blood spatter**. CSIs study the patterns. They can learn where people were during a crime.

bullet—a small, pointed metal object fired from a gun

blood spatter—a pattern of blood drops of various sizes

Each spatter pattern can give investigators clues.

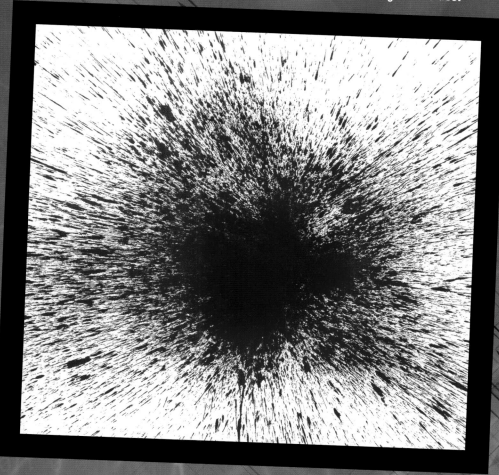

FACT

A criminal may take an object from a crime scene.
This can leave an open spot in blood spatter called a void.

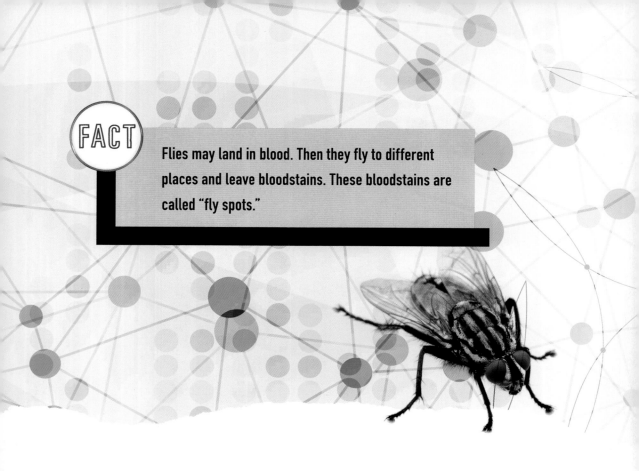

Flies may land in blood. Then they fly to different places and leave bloodstains. These bloodstains are called "fly spots."

Weapons leave different bloodstain patterns. CSIs know what pattern each weapon leaves behind. The patterns help them guess which weapons were used in a crime.

CSIs can also study wounds to help them learn
how a weapon was used in a crime.

CHAPTER 4

USING BLOOD EVIDENCE

Scientists can do **DNA** tests on crime-scene blood. They enter DNA information into **databases**. The databases hold DNA records of criminals. Computers search for matches to the crime-scene blood.

DNA—material in cells that gives people their individual characteristics; DNA stands for deoxyribonucleic acid

database—a collection of organized information on a computer

All people share 99.98 percent of the same DNA. But only identical twins have the exact same DNA.

A scientist removes a DNA sample stick from a tube during testing.

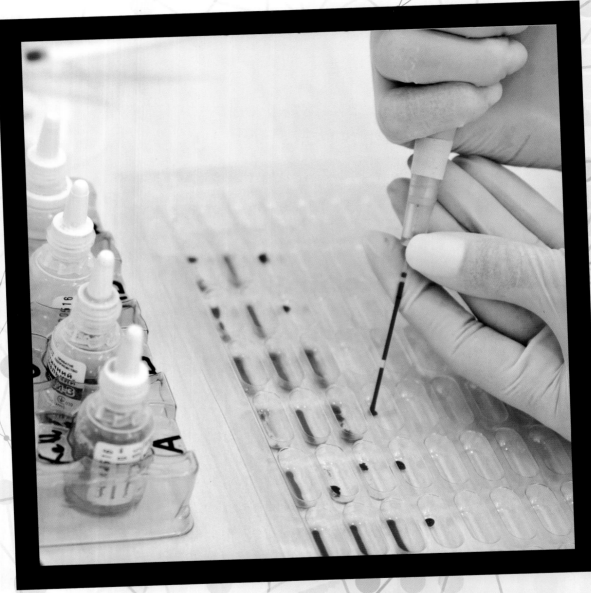

A scientist performs a test for blood type.

Sometimes DNA tests can't be done. Lab workers then check the blood type of a sample from a crime scene. Each person's blood type is A, B, AB, or O. CSIs can see if it matches a **suspect's** blood type.

FACT

Animals have blood types too. Cats have three. Horses have eight. Dogs have 13 different blood types.

suspect—someone thought to be responsible for a crime

Blood evidence can be very helpful in court. DNA testing is 99 percent accurate. Just one drop of blood can help solve a crime.

FACT

DNA testing has proven that people found guilty of crimes were actually **innocent**. In the United States, it has proven the innocence of more than 350 people.

innocent—not guilty

An expert explains DNA evidence in court.

GLOSSARY

blood spatter (BLUHD SPAT-ur)—a pattern of blood drops of various sizes

bullet (BU-luht)—a small, pointed metal object fired from a gun

chemical (KE-muh-kuhl)—a substance used in or produced by chemistry; medicines, gunpowder, and food preservatives all are made from chemicals

criminal (KRI-muh-nuhl)—someone who commits a crime

crown (KRAUN)—a jagged edge on a blood drop

database (DAY-tuh-bays)—a collection of organized information on a computer

DNA (dee-en-AY)—material in cells that gives people their individual characteristics; DNA stands for deoxyribonucleic acid

evidence (EHV-uh-duhns)—information, items, and facts that help prove something is true or false; criminal evidence can be used in court cases

innocent (IN-uh-suhnt)—not guilty

record (ree-KORD)—to show evidence of something

scene (SEEN)—the place of an event or action

suspect (SUHSS-spekt)—someone thought to be responsible for a crime

victim (VIK-tuhm)—a person who is hurt, killed, or made to suffer because of a disaster, accident, or crime

READ MORE

Carmichael, L. E. *Discover Forensic Science.* What's Cool About Science? Minneapolis: Lerner Publications, 2017.

Korté, Steve. *The Spitting Image: Batman and Robin Use DNA Analysis to Crack the Case.* Batman & Robin Crime Scene Investigations. North Mankato, Minn.: Capstone, 2017.

Orr, Tamra. *Crime Scene Investigator.* Cool STEAM Careers. Ann Arbor, Mich.: Cherry Lake Publishing, 2016.

INTERNET SITES

Use FactHound to find Internet sites related to this book.

Visit *www.facthound.com*

Just type in **9781543529876** and go.

Check out projects, games and lots more at
www.capstonekids.com

CRITICAL THINKING QUESTIONS

1. CSIs must collect blood evidence correctly. What do you think could happen if they didn't collect it properly?

2. How can CSIs tell if blood is from a moving person? How can they tell it is from a person who is not moving?

3. Sometimes CSIs can't see blood at a crime scene. What are some ways CSIs can make the blood appear? Use online and other sources to compare the disadvantages and advantages of two different methods.

INDEX

blood spatter, 20, 21
bloodstain patterns, 16, 20, 22
blood types, 27

chemicals, 8, 11, 12
cotton swabs, 7, 11, 14
court, 28
crowns, 16

databases, 24
DNA tests, 24, 27, 28

fly spots, 22

lights, 11, 12
luminol, 12

pictures, 14

tails, 19
transfer bloodstains, 9

weapons, 22